First Science

Colorful Light

Editorial planning: Serpentine Editorial
Scientific consultant: Dr. J.J.M. Rowe

Designed by The R & B Partnership
Illustrator: David Anstey
Photographer: Peter Millard

Additional photographs:
Chris Fairclough Colour Library 6, 20, 30 (top and bottom);
ZEFA 16, 19 (bottom);
The Hutchison Library 19 (top);
Eye Ubiquitous 29.

Library of Congress Cataloging-in-Publication Data

Rowe, Julian.
    Colorful light / by Julian Rowe and Molly Perham.
      p.   cm. — (First science)
    Includes index.
    Summary: Describes in simple terms different aspects of color and light
including rainbows, bubbles, warning colors, camouflage, and reflections.
    ISBN 0-516-08131-4
      1. Color—Experiments—Juvenile literature. 2. Light—Experiments—Juvenile
literature. [1. Color—Experiments. 2. Light—Experiments. 3. Experiments.]
    I. Perham, Molly. II. Title. III. Series: First science (Chicago, Ill.)
    QC495.5.R69 1993
    535'.078—dc20   93-8217
                                                                              CIP
                                                                               AC

First Science

Colorful Light

Julian Rowe
and Molly Perham

CHILDRENS PRESS®

CHICAGO

Contents

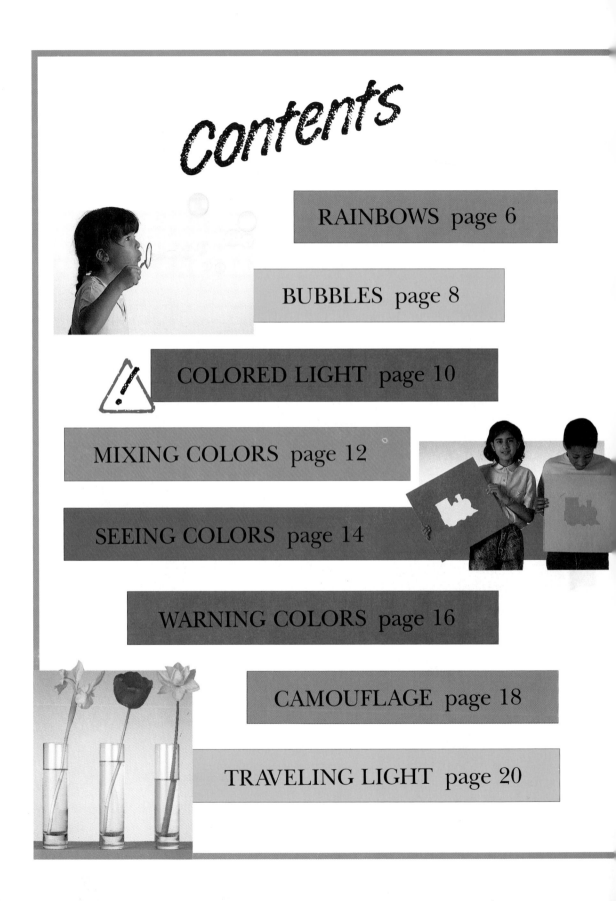

SAFETY WARNING

Activities marked with this symbol require the presence and help of an adult. Plastic should always be used instead of glass.

Rainbows

Have you seen a rainbow? When the sun shines on a rainy day an arch of bright colors appears in the sky.

How many colors can you see in this rainbow?

Make a Rainbow

Materials: A glass,
a mirror made of
plastic, and a sheet
of white paper.

Fill the glass with water.
Stand the glass on the
paper near a window.

Put the mirror in
the glass.

Move the glass so
that sunlight shines
through the water
onto the mirror.

Can you see a rainbow on the paper?

Bubbles

The sunlight that shines through the window is made up of many colors.

In a rainbow you can see each color by itself. When light strikes a tiny drop of water, it splits into different colors.

Can you see rainbow colors in these bubbles?

Blowing bubbles

Materials: Bubble mix.
Blow big and small
bubbles.
Do they all have
rainbow colors?
Where do the
colors come
from?

Where else do you
see rainbow colors?

Colored light

If you mix all the colors of the rainbow together, you make white light.

If you mix two or more colors, you make colored light. In this picture red, green, and blue lights make different-colored shadows on the wall.

Materials: A piece
of white cardboard,
a glass, scissors,
a pencil, and some
crayons or paints.

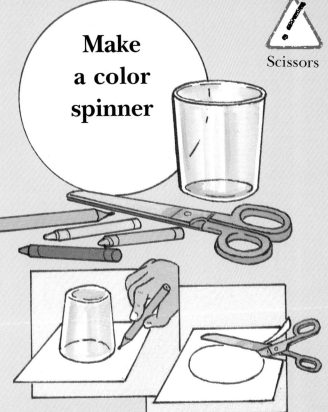

**Make
a color
spinner**

Scissors

Stand the glass on
the white cardboard
and trace around it.
Ask an adult to help
you cut out the
circle.

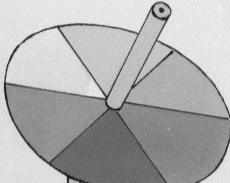

Draw six equal
sections on the card.
Color each one a
color of the rainbow.

Make a hole in the
middle of the card.
Stick a pencil
through it.

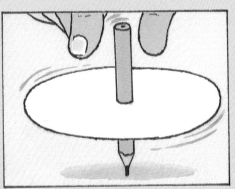

Now try spinning your color spinner.
What color is it when it is spinning fast?

Mixing colors

Paints and colored things contain pigments.
Pigments take in, or absorb, some of
the colors in light. The color you see
is sent back, or reflected.

Why do you think an object looks
blue, or yellow,
or green?

Try mixing colors with your paints.
Mixing paints is not the same as mixing
colored lights. What happens if you mix
all the colors together?

Yellow and blue
make green.

Red and blue
make purple.

Red and yellow
make orange.

Blue, red, and yellow
make dark brown.

Seeing colors

This paper looks green. It absorbs all the colors in the white light shining on it except the green light.

We see the green color that is reflected into our eyes. Grass looks green because it reflects green light.

Look at the pictures
these children are
holding. Which train
stands out best against
the background?

Warning colors

Some colors are easier to see than others. Bright colors are useful warning signals.

The yellow color of this frog warns other animals that it is poisonous. Fire trucks are red so that everyone can see them clearly and get out of the way.

When you go out walking it is a good idea to wear brightly colored clothes. They stand out against the green and brown background of the countryside.

People will find you more easily if you get lost.

Camouflage

Bird-watchers wear colored clothes that cannot easily be seen against the bushes and trees. This disguise, or camouflage, allows them to get close to birds without disturbing them.

Many animals have colors that match their surroundings. These colors help to camouflage the animals and protect them against enemies.

The chameleon (above) can change the color of its skin to match its surroundings.

This moth on the right is not easy to see when it rests on the bark of a tree.

Traveling light

Light travels in straight lines. It does not bend around things. Look at these rays of sunlight shining through the trees.

Light travels more slowly through glass and water than it does through air. When a ray of light travels from air through water it changes direction. This makes these flower stems look broken.

Shadows

A solid object does not let light travel through it. It casts a shadow. A shadow is made where most of the light cannot reach.

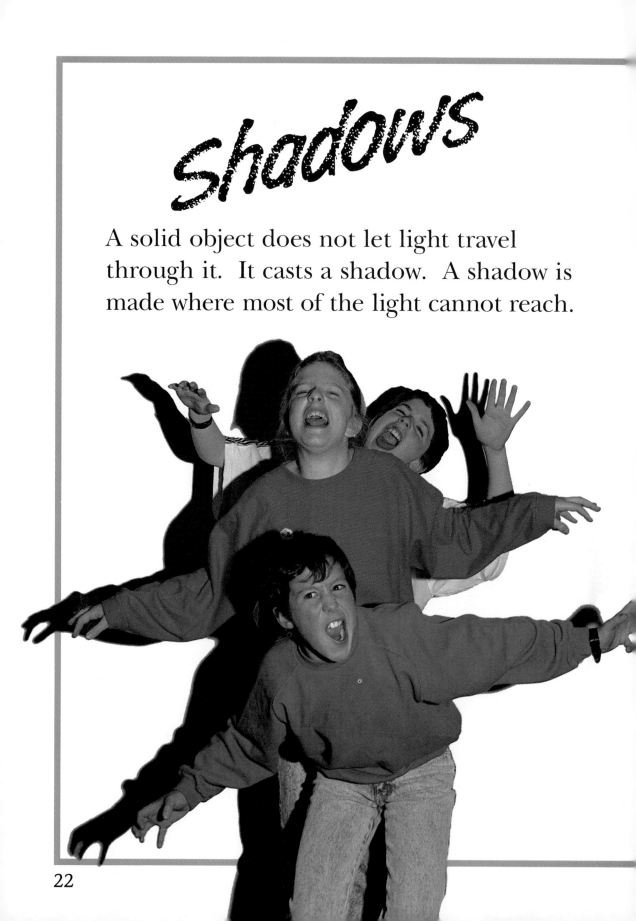

Can you see which objects made these shadows?

Bouncing back

Some materials reflect more light than others. The smooth, flat shiny surface of a mirror reflects nearly all of the light. A rough, dark surface hardly reflects any light.

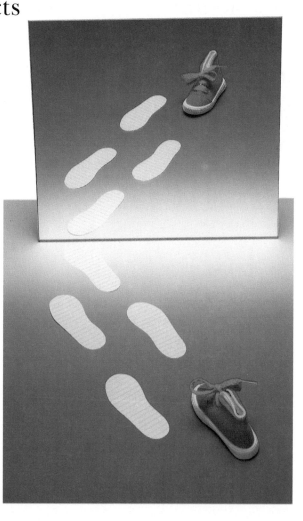

See how the shoe and the four footprints are reflected in the mirror.

A shape that is exactly the same on both sides is called symmetrical. When you hold a mirror along the center of it, you see the whole object.

What happens if you hold a mirror against each of these pictures?

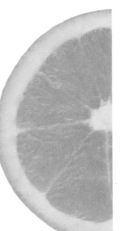

Reflections

The real clock looks different from the reflection you see in the mirror.
Can you see how it is different?

The reflection is backward. The numbers have changed sides. You can't read the numbers.

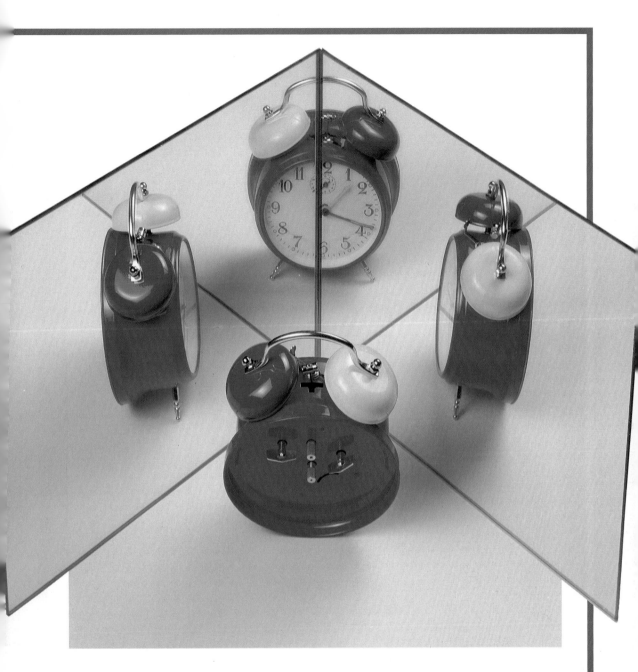

What happens if you hold two mirrors at an angle in front of the clock? Now the reflection in one mirror is facing front. Can you figure out why this happens?

Funny faces

Look at your reflection in a big spoon.

The back of the spoon bulges outward. Look at your reflection in the back of the spoon. It looks small!

The bowl of the spoon is hollow. Your reflection in the bowl looks much bigger. But which way is up?

Curved mirrors change the size and shape of objects that are reflected in them. Mirrors with lots of curves make very funny reflections.

Think about... light

This is a full moon. It looks very bright in the clear sky at night. But the moon has no light of its own. It simply reflects the light of the sun.

A blind person uses touch to read the Braille marks on the page. Blind people can read without light.

A cat can see better in the dark than you can. Its eyes are sensitive to light you cannot see. Cats can hunt their prey in the dark.

Face the light from the window. NEVER look directly at the sun. Ask a friend to look into your eyes. Are your pupils big or small? Then look into a dark closet.

What size are your pupils?

Large pupils let in more light, so you can see better.